# CORNWALL

PETER LANYON   DRAWINGS · PHOTOGRAPHS   ANDREW LANYON

# Introduction

' "It's always that gorgeous blue on the Cornish coast", said Dick.' The words are Enid Blyton's, of course: her Cornish clichés. 'Tremannon' in *Five Go Down To The Sea* comes straight off a GWR poster. 'Caves—and more caves—and yet more caves! And cove after cove, all as lovely as the one before.' Blyton's Cornwall is a background where only the cliffs frown: tourist Cornwall without the tourists.

The Lanyons' Cornwall too is riddled with coves, but not cupcake coves. Some are choked with boulders. There are messy tidelines, rockfalls, decrepit harbours, oil slicks scabbing the water. The sky, more often than not, is overcast. The landscape, D. H. Lawrence wrote, 'is bare and dark and elemental'. Maybe so but it is also lived in, worked over, crowded with associations, strung with barbed wire and telephone lines.

The drawings and photographs in this book are a combined celebration of Cornwall itself—Lyonesse turned Lanyonesse—and of continuity. Peter Lanyon died as a result of a gliding accident when his son Andrew was seventeen, in 1964. As the drawings ended, the photographs began. Put together on facing pages they form sequences and relay themes. Photographically-reproduced drawings are shadows of the originals. You miss the feel of the paper, the scratches and the whiffs of colour, the sketchbook urgency, the precise scale. Reproduced photographs too are rendered somewhat uniform; nuances are inevitably lost in the printing. So to some extent both bodies of work are compromised on this neutral ground. Together though they add up to a marvellous account of the Cornwall that lies behind the clichés.

Looking at photographs is a way of seeing at second hand. Drawings are more direct (eye to hand to eye) yet often more difficult to make out; for while photographs register, drawings are reactions. That's the basic difference: the glancing line as opposed to the arrested wave.

During his time at Zennor (when locals of a Famous Five disposition assumed him to be a German spy) Lawrence wrote, 'I lie looking down at a cove where the waves come white under a low, black headland, which slopes up in bare green-brown, bare and sad under a level sky.' He turned landscape into recitative, blending topography, history and mood. 'It is old, Celtic, pre-Christian. Tristan and his boat, and his horn.' Looking down at Church Cove, Gunwalloe, Peter Lanyon probably took only thirty seconds to note the building, scribble the bushes round the churchyard, the dim bulk of the headland, the sluicing waves. The drawing is little more than a memo. 'I have to refer back continually to what is under my feet, to what is over my back, to what I see in front of me.' Lanyon used to urge his students to lie on their backs, 'look at the sky and *feel*'. The cliff-top sensation, of pressing oneself to the ground, watching the clouds move, feeling the world turn, becomes the graveyard experience of imagining past generations of Cornishmen, beached in their coffins beside the cove, rising up and putting out to sea with the tide. 'Tristan and his boat, and his horn.'

Andrew Lanyon's photograph of the same place leaves less to the imagination. He placed himself in a commanding position, overlooking the three saw-toothed roofs, the detached tower, like a squat obelisk, the cars on the far slope above the cliffs, the lunge and explosion of the breakers, the dull winter sky. Seen together the drawing and the photograph re-echo. Peter Lanyon takes the lead, Andrew follows suit. The motif they share is land and sea: tidal time and motionless terrain. 'A fierce coast and a hungry sea', is how Enid Blyton put it. That's the picture-postcard view. The Lanyons not only avoid the obvious stances they ignore the picturesque. Theirs is a Cornwall out of season when nothing can be glossed over.

Construction for St Just, 1952.
Glass, paint and bostik, 23 × 10 × 9.

Again and again themes defined by the father find further expression in the son's isolated images. Peter Lanyon would cast around before attempting to synthesize. 'I wanted to bring together all my feelings about the landscape, and this meant breaking away from the visual method of representing space in a landscape painting—receding like a cone to a vanishing point. I wanted to find a new way of organizing the space in a picture.' He learned from Alfred Wallis, the St Ives primitive, how to dispense with conventional perspective. If you ignored it, the pressure to represent scenes as peepshows disappeared. Lanyon drew St Ives harbour in the Wallis manner, houses like pop-up cut-outs, boats dumped at all angles, people standing by like exclamation marks. From Naum Gabo and Ben Nicholson he learned the ruthless, pattern-maker's art of fitting form to format, striving always for decisive qualities, for high-handed clarity. But he added his rider: a painting is nothing, he said, 'unless it is constructed out of experience and returns to experience'.

*St Just*, of 1952–3, is a good example of what he was after and what he accomplished. 'St Just is the last town in England before you reach Land's End. It's an old mining town, with disused mine shafts all around it.' He wanted to paint not the scene—an overall view, say—but the entire place as he had experienced it over the years. 'The place complete, with all its associations.'

This involved making drawings of the church tower, of the telegraph poles, fields, houses, the lie of the land. Then, he said, 'before making the painting I began to crystallize my experience of the landscape into an object made out of sheets of glass painted and stuck together. What happens here is mostly to do with mining—the pithead gear of the mine, the shaft itself, the lodes of tin.' The painting, filtered through mock-ups and experience, emerged as a vertical mass, laid out and exposed like a pelt nailed to a barn door. Horizons stretch along all four margins. The centre is a black gash, a sheer drop, to be read as shaft or main road, the backbone of the community.

In the painting Lanyon could both restructure his experience and clothe it, laying down rib-cage field systems, smearing the bedrock with grass, providing hectic atmosphere and cloud cover. Retracing his steps, reverting to the preliminary drawings, it becomes obvious that the vital move, the reorientation, was the ascent from ground level to that hovering, all-embracing vantage point where his world shrank into a target. The drawings are pointers only.

Lanyon would describe himself, with perhaps mock modesty, as a minor provincial landscape painter. He died before he had the chance to spend extended periods elsewhere. He was, apart from a few forays, a Cornish painter. What in other, happier circumstances, might have proved to have been just his Cornish period, turned out to be virtually his whole life. Had he moved on, the localities that he knew better than any other St Ives School painter would have receded. But rather than speculate on what might have been, it is surely better to appreciate what this 'minor provincial' actually achieved.

All good landscape painting is the work not of the traveller but of the inhabitant. It has to be provincial. For the topographer deals in neat accounts of places. Edward Lear treated everywhere the same. Turner processed everywhere into the same rarefied turbulences. The true landscapist, whether a Constable or a Cézanne, is rarely at home, so to speak, in more than one place. Lose sight of your roots and you become displaced and relatively superficial. Superstitions accrue around this assumption, and staying put can become an excuse for vegetating. But with Peter Lanyon the possibilities opened up only when he cultivated what he really knew. 'I had to accept the fact against my will; that I

St Just, 1952–3. Oil, 96 × 48.

functioned best when concerned with my immediate environment.'

Spying out the ground, walking the coast, climbing Rosewall Hill, the Lanyons were on the look-out. For Peter Lanyon drawing was a matter of keeping his hand in and thinking on paper. For Andrew Lanyon photography isn't an art to be pursued with lofty self-esteem but a means of seizing chances and fixing things. For both of them the object was always to make things clear.

Each of the photographs is an observation; most of them convey the peninsular conditions of exposed fronts and prevailing winds. Ivy teased into a bouffant growth on the end of an outbuilding, hair blowing wildly, starlings peppering the sky, cricketers playing on despite heavy mist. The cottage-loaf fissures in rocks, the nest of stones on a foreshore, the monkey-puzzle tree counterpointing the black rafters of an abandoned dwelling, gorse and vapour trails, a horse turning its head to face the dark drum of what the architectural guides would call a vernacular building.

Cornwall has new attractions besides cove after cove and well-advertised Ancient Stones. You can 'Take the Family Underground at Poldark Mine', see for yourself 'The Mystery of Cornish Tin' at Redruth, explore 'Flambards Village' at the Cornwall Aero-Park. A century ago Newlyn was the place where the artists settled in order to paint fisherfolk. Now with unemployment worse than ever, with fishing in decline and mining near-extinct, the tendency is to turn useful activities into leisure complexes. Peter Lanyon talked of the pernicious effect of the preservationists and beautifiers. 'Generations of Cornishmen have had to leave their native coast and have died in exile, leaving only a chimney as their monument. When the new-arrived see the revenge of time creep up on their doorsteps, they wail out that we destroy the beauty of their views. What view do they think the Cornishman has, who desires above all to make his own riches, but is barred by some concept of beauty that denies him the honour of his labour?'

Lanyon was objecting to those who objected to plans for opening a mine at Carnelloe near Zennor in 1961. His argument is that of the inhabitant rather than the lover of the 'unspoilt' or the picturesque. To him Cornwall was a constant, not an Area of Outstanding Beauty. This is what kept him from being a complacent minor provincial landscape painter, a purveyor of Cornish clichés. His drawings are his response to what lay around him. His paintings take things further. Porthleven rears up and discloses itself, inner harbour, outer harbour, terraces, clock-tower; Portreath coils in on itself, bleached to the bone.

Few people appear in either the drawings or the photographs. They are busy elsewhere. Also, in the drawings and paintings anyway, figures would be inappropriate for throughout Peter Lanyon's work there runs a streak of anthropomorphic zeal: the desire to see landscape as a responsive body. Cornwall lies stroked and tugged at by the sea, offering shelter in her inlets, security in her folds. *St Just* can be taken for a crucifixion. *Porthleven* can be interpreted as a pair of gossiping fishwives, the sort Frank Bramley or Stanhope Forbes liked to paint in the heyday of the Newlyn School. When Lanyon reconnoitred he eliminated incidentals: standing stones, a horse, a rook or a gull counted for more than the average intruder. Lack of people emphasize the Lawrentian quality. 'It is not England. It is bare and dark and elemental, Tristan's land.' The main sensation is of isolation, yourself alone, gulls screaming, wind interfering, a beleaguered state.

The lines of each drawing plunge across the contours, burrow into hollows, wriggle along crevices, stream into the sky. They change direction, turn contradictory, cancel out. Most of all, they define. As Daniel Defoe said of Boscawen-Ûn stone circle, 'all that can be learn'd of them is, that *here they are*'. Lanyon proceeds like a dowser, across country, probing sensitive spots. It was only later, in the studio, that he could hope to make sense of what he set down in such conditions, at such a speed. The drawings are skirmishes; their implications were brought out in the paintings.

The Cornwall of fudge, cream, pixy charms and freezer centres is too trivial to be worth recording here. Both Lanyons deal in myths: Peter concerning himself with 'seasonal myth about the seed lying in the earth during the winter and coming back to life in the spring', Andrew delving into antiquarian byways and local folklore. The drawings tie the elements together, Mother Cornwall—Ancient Cornwall—the Underworld where the tin lodes lay, the landmarks (Lanyon Quoit), the dereliction. The photographs are more anecdotal, more as-it-happened. They play on incongruities (the ship out of water, the solid shadow against the insubstantial wall) and on the idea of Cornwall as an extremity littered with leftovers. The wit lies in the omissions: Cornwall made unobvious.

WILLIAM FEAVER

Gunwalloe Cove, *c*. 1959. Charcoal, 14 × 10.

Gunwalloe, 1967.

12

Boscastle, 1956. Charcoal, 20 × 16.

Godrevy, December 1967.

Walls and bird, 1963. Crayon, 15 × 20.

Hedge above Zennor.

Study for Mullion Bay IV, 1954. Charcoal, 15 × 20.

Madron.

Redruth, *c.* 1953. Charcoal, $11\frac{1}{4} \times 13\frac{3}{4}$.

West Penwith.

Portreath Rock, 1950. Gouache, $10 \times 13\frac{1}{2}$.

Lanyon Quoit.

Godolphin Hill from Rock Close Wood, $11 \times 16\frac{1}{2}$.

Rosewall Hill.

Portreath study. Pencil, charcoal and gouache, 10 × 14.

Nine Maidens, Gurnard's Head, April 1968.

Cape Cornwall, 1952. Charcoal and pencil, $9\frac{3}{4} \times 12$.

Levant Mine ruins, 1963. Charcoal, 14 × 10.

Harbour, 1946. Incised line, $10\frac{3}{4} \times 13\frac{1}{2}$.

Wreck of Victoire Roger of Ostend at Land's End, March 1964.

Landscape on a visiting card, 1963. Crayon, $1\frac{3}{4} \times 3$.

Oil slick from the Torrey Canyon near Land's End, 1967.

32

Chapel near Camborne. Incised line, $12\frac{1}{4} \times 10\frac{1}{4}$.

Farm buildings near St Day, 1965.

Starlings at dusk near Marazion.

1969.

St Just, 1952. Pencil, $10\frac{3}{4} \times 15$.

St Just, September 1966.

Mines behind Camborne, 1953. Charcoal, 16 × 20.

Penzance, 1965.

Porthleven, 1950. Charcoal, 22 × 15.

Cricket in the mist near St Ives, 1969.

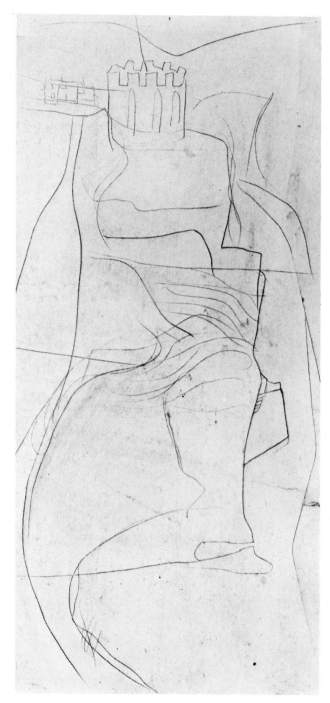

Cliff tower, 1955. Incised line, $13\frac{3}{4} \times 6\frac{1}{4}$.

Boscawen-Ûn Circle.

Houses at Cape Cornwall, 1946. Pencil, $9\frac{1}{4} \times 12$.

Old mines, Pool, 1953. Charcoal, 16 × 20.

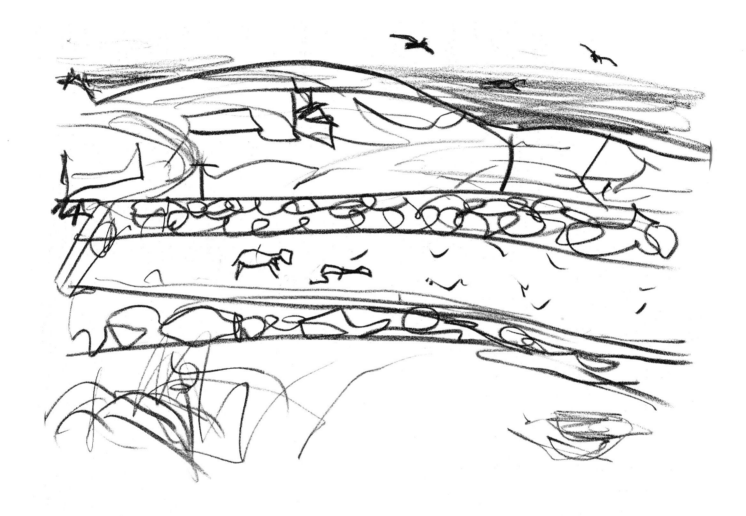

Walls and fields, 1963. Crayon, 15 × 20.

Coal being loaded into a lorry near Carn Brea, 1966.

Study of cliffs, 1950. Crayon, 10×15.

Clay tip, 1966.

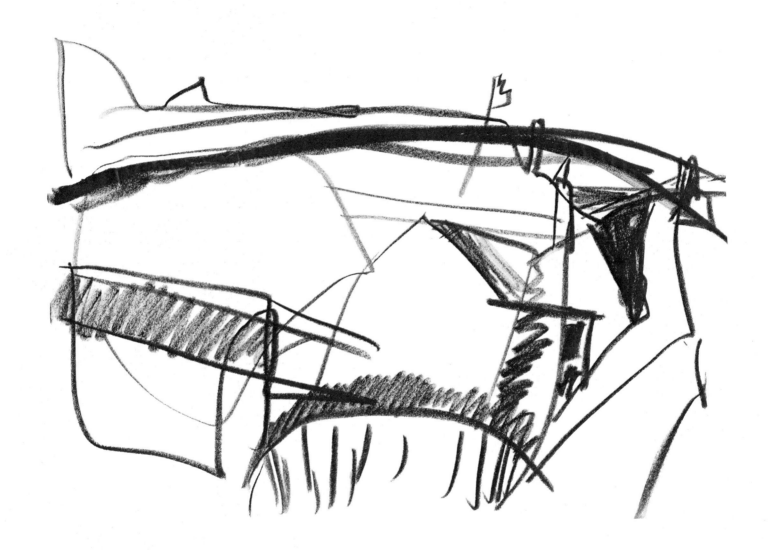

*Coast near Newquay, 1964. Crayon, 15 × 20.*

Zennor, April 1970.

Portreath Bay, 1951. Charcoal.

Zennor, April 1970.

Mine drawing, 1963. Charcoal, $9\frac{3}{4} \times 14$.

Ding Dong.

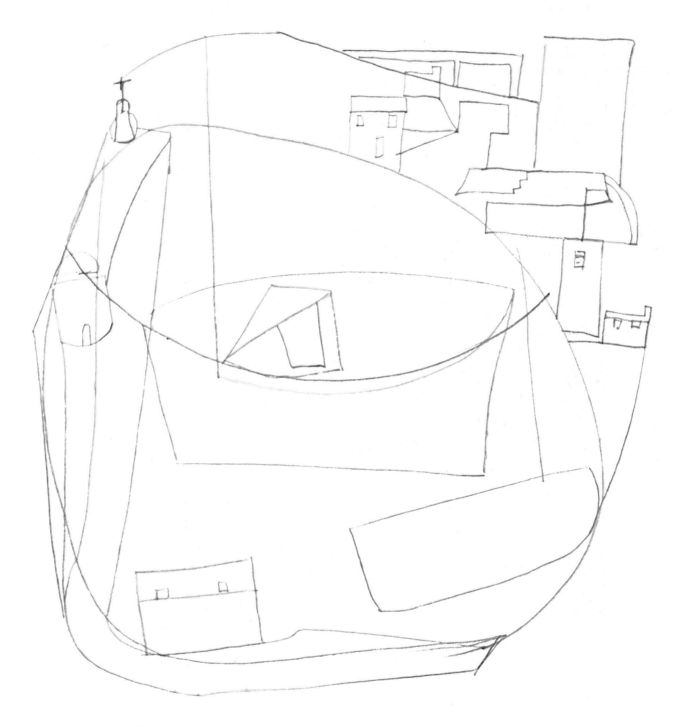

St Ives harbour, *c.* 1946. Pencil, $7\frac{1}{2} \times 8$.

Near Man's Head, St Ives, 1969.

Horse near Lanyon Quoit.

Sennen Round House.

Wheelbarrow, Little Park Owles, Carbis Bay, 1955. Etching, $9\frac{1}{4} \times 7\frac{1}{4}$.

Study for Porthleven, 1950. Charcoal, 9½ × 13.

Mousehole harbour, 1956.

Walls at Porthmeor near Zennor.

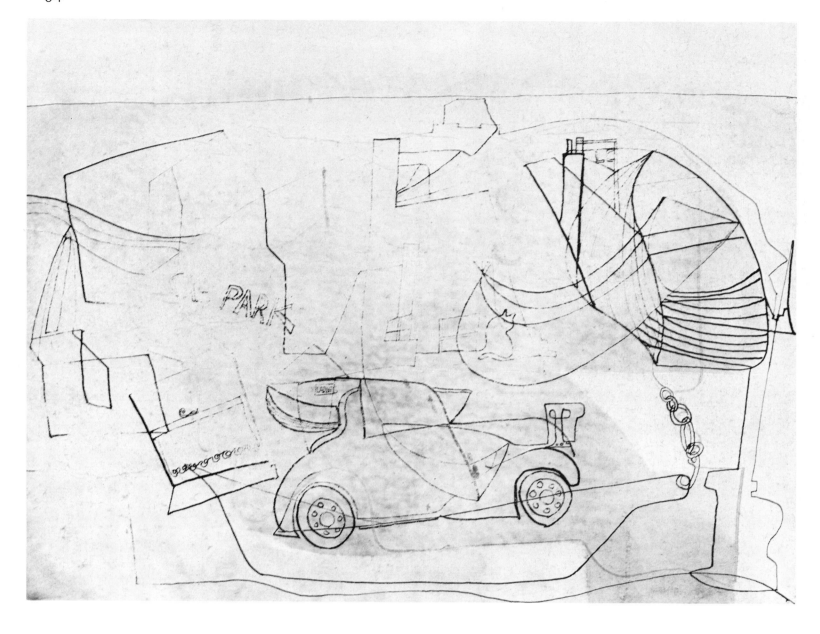

St Ives, 1946. Pen and watercolour, $9\frac{3}{4} \times 12\frac{3}{4}$.

Near Padstow, May Day 1971.

Study for Mullion
Bay II, 1954.
Charcoal and
pencil, $11\frac{3}{4} \times 9\frac{1}{2}$.

Cot Valley.

Study for Mullion Bay III, 1954. Charcoal and pencil, $11\frac{1}{2} \times 14$.

1966.

Study for St Just, *c.* 1951. Charcoal and pencil, $9\frac{3}{4} \times 13\frac{1}{4}$.

St Just.

Porthleven, 1950. Charcoal, 15 × 22.

GWR near Demelza.

Godrevy, 1960.

Whitesand Bay, Sennen, April 1968.

St Ives harbour, *c.* 1946. Ink on windowblind canvas, $17 \times 19\frac{3}{4}$.

Spraying Torrey Canyon oil with detergent at Porthleven, 1967.

## PETER LANYON

Peter Lanyon was born in 1918 in St Ives, the son of WH Lanyon, musician and amateur photographer. In 1936 he received tuition from Borlase Smart and in 1939 from Ben Nicholson. He studied at Penzance School of Art and for four months at the Euston Road School.

In 1937 he met Adrian Stokes whose book *Colour and Form* particularly influenced him, as did the work of Naum Gabo who in 1939 was living near St Ives in Carbis Bay.

During the war he served in the RAF as an aero-engine fitter in the Western Desert and Italy, returning to the latter country in 1948, 1957 and 1962. Apart from the war years and brief visits to South Africa, Holland, Aix-en-Provence, New York, Texas and Czechoslovakia, he spent most of his life within a mile or so of where he was born in St Ives.

His first London exhibition was at the Lefevre Gallery in 1949. He taught at Bath Academy of Art, Corsham, from 1950 to 1957, then at St Peter's Loft, St Ives from 1957 to 1960.

In 1954 he received the Critic's prize and in 1959 John Moore's second prize. A Marzotto award in 1962 enabled him to paint in Anticoli Corrado, Italy.

In 1959 he started gliding and began to re-explore the landscape he knew so well from the ground. In 1964, after a gliding accident, he died.

Peter Lanyon gliding at Perranporth, 1963.

ANDREW LANYON

Andrew Lanyon was born in 1947. An early leaning towards the church was swiftly averted when, after he was spotted genuflecting in a lane near a convent school in Hayle, his father intervened. He was sent to a girls' school in Woking where he remembers going on long nature walks. Graduating to a boys' school he won a camera in a comic competition and soon took up the dark cloth and disappeared into a water tank his father had converted into a darkroom.

An interest in conjuring led to some disastrous live performances and taught him it was safer to perpetrate trickery from a distance. Trick photography led eventually to portraiture, for which he used his grandfather's plate camera, and then genre and reportage after he received a travel scholarship from Bryanston School to circle England with his Periflex.

At sixteen he fell in love with an early Leica in a Bond Street window and went heavily into debt. Another travel scholarship enabled him to visit Paris in 1964 and, perfecting his hidden Leica technique, he caught Parisians unawares—or some, for he narrowly escaped death by prostitute when attacked by a number near Les Halles. On another occasion his camera was wrenched from him and would have been dashed to pieces had not an associate with unusual presence of mind explained it was not a camera but a device for testing the intensity of street lighting for the local council. While in Paris he met Man Ray and took a series of photographs of a suicide from the Eiffel Tower which led to some part-time work for the *Daily Express*.

Back at home in Cornwall and London, where he attended the London School of Film Technique in 1966, he cruised the lanes and streets Cartier Bresson-fashion, perfecting invisibility, stalking his prey with the stealth of a panther and the innocence of a ventriloquist.

However, after seven years of squinting through a viewfinder, his left eye jammed. Headaches, combined with a desire to tamper with the image led to a steady decline to photomontage, collage and finally, in 1971, painting.

**Owners of Drawings**
Mr and Mrs Peter Garlake, p. 5 (St Just, oil); Anthony Diamond, p. 12; Keir McGuinness, p. 18; Andrew Lanyon, pp. 20, 32, 60; Bret Guthrie, p. 22; Mrs Cornel Lucas, p. 42; British Museum Department of Prints and Drawings, p. 45; William Feaver, p. 48; owner unknown, p. 52; Arthur Caddick, p. 62; City of Stoke-on-Trent Museum and Art Gallery, p. 70; Robert and Christine Hopper, p. 74; others owned by Sheila Lanyon.

**Note on the Pictures**
Measurements of drawings are given in inches, height before width.
　　The photographs were taken on Kodak Plus-X film, with an early Leica fitted with an Elmar 3.5 lens, and were printed on Agfa Portriga Rapid paper.

This book has been published in conjunction with an exhibition of the drawings and photographs of Cornwall by Peter Lanyon and Andrew Lanyon, financially assisted by the British Council.

First published in 1983 by
Alison Hodge
Bosulval Farmhouse, Newmill,
Penzance, Cornwall.

© Introduction, William Feaver, 1983
© Andrew Lanyon, 1983
Designer: Stuart Hamilton

ISBN 0 906720 06 0

Printed in Great Britain by
BAS Printers Ltd.,
Over Wallop, Stockbridge, Hampshire.